THE COLOR PURPLE

Alice Walker

TECHNICAL DIRECTOR Maxwell Krohn
EDITORIAL DIRECTOR Justin Kestler
MANAGING EDITOR Ben Florman

SERIES EDITORS Boomie Aglietti, Justin Kestler
PRODUCTION Christian Lorentzen

WRITERS Brenna Moore, Selena Ward
EDITORS Matt Blanchard, Sarah Friedberg

This edition published by Spark Publishing

Spark Publishing
A Division of SparkNotes LLC
120 Fifth Avenue, 8th Floor
New York, NY 10011

02 03 04 05 SN 9 8 7 6 5 4 3 2 1

Please send all comments and questions or report errors to
feedback@sparknotes.com.

Library of Congress information available upon request

Printed and bound in the United States

RRD-C

ISBN 1-58663-448-8

Introduction:
Stopping to
Buy SparkNotes
on a
Snowy Evening

Whose words these are you *think* you know.
Your paper's due tomorrow, though;
We're glad to see you stopping here
To get some help before you go.

Lost your course? You'll find it here.
Face tests and essays without fear.
Between the words, good grades at stake:
Get great results throughout the year.

Once school bells caused your heart to quake
As teachers circled each mistake.
Use SparkNotes and no longer weep,
Ace every single test you take.

Yes, books are lovely, dark, and deep,
But only what you grasp you keep,
With hours to go before you sleep,
With hours to go before you sleep.

CONTENTS

CONTEXT

ALICE WALKER WAS BORN on February 9, 1944, in the small rural town of Eatonton, Georgia. She was the eighth and last child of Willie Lee Walker and Minnie Tallulah Grant, two sharecroppers. Walker's parents' experiences with the oppressive sharecropping system and the racism of the American South deeply influenced Walker's writing and life's work. When Walker was eight, one of her brothers accidentally shot her, permanently blinding her in one eye. Ashamed of her facial disfigurement, Walker isolated herself from other children, reading and writing to pass the time.

In 1961, on a scholarship for disabled students, Walker enrolled in Spelman College in Atlanta, where she became active in the African-American civil rights movement. Two years later, Walker transferred to Sarah Lawrence College in New York and eventually traveled to Uganda as an exchange student. When she returned for her senior year, Walker was shocked to learn that she was pregnant, and, afraid of her parents' reaction, she considered suicide. However, a classmate helped Walker obtain a safe abortion, and she graduated from Sarah Lawrence in 1965. At this time, Walker composed two early landmark pieces: "To Hell with Dying," her first published short story, and *Once: Poems*, her first volume of poetry.

Walker continued her involvement with the civil rights movement after graduation, working as a volunteer on black voter registration drives in Georgia and Mississippi in 1965 and 1966. In 1967, Walker married Melvyn Leventhal, a Jewish civil rights lawyer, with whom she had one daughter before the two divorced in the mid-1970s. Walker's second novel, *Meridian*, explored the controversial issue of sexism in the civil rights movement.

In 1982, Walker published her most famous novel, *The Color Purple*. For the novel, which chronicles the struggle of several black women in rural Georgia in the first half of the twentieth century, Walker won the Pulitzer Prize and the American Book Award. In 1985, a Steven Spielberg film based on the novel was released to wide audiences and significant acclaim.

Upon its publication, *The Color Purple* unleashed a storm of controversy. It instigated heated debates about black cultural representation, as a number of male African-American critics complained that the novel reaffirmed old racist stereotypes about pathology in black communities and of black men in particular. Critics also charged Walker with focusing heavily on sexism at the expense of addressing notions of racism in America. Nonetheless, *The Color Purple* also had its ardent supporters, especially among black women and others who praised the novel as a feminist fable. The heated disputes surrounding *The Color Purple* are a testimony to the resounding effects the work has had on cultural and racial discourse in the United States.

Walker's 1992 novel, *Possessing the Secret of Joy,* concerns the marriage of Adam and Tashi—two characters who make their first appearance in *The Color Purple*—and the consequences of Tashi's decision to undergo the traditional African ritual of female circumcision. Walker has continued to explore the unique problems that face black women in both in the United States and Africa. Her novels, poetry, essays, and criticism have become an important part in a burgeoning tradition of talented black women writers.

Plot Overview

ELIE, THE PROTAGONIST AND NARRATOR of *The Color Purple*, is a poor, uneducated, fourteen-year-old black girl living in rural Georgia. Celie starts writing letters to God because her father, Alphonso, beats and rapes her. Alphonso has already impregnated Celie once. Celie gave birth to a girl, whom her father stole and presumably killed in the woods. Celie has a second child, a boy, whom her father also steals. Celie's mother becomes seriously ill and dies. Alphonso brings home a new wife but continues to abuse Celie.

Celie and her bright, pretty younger sister, Nettie, learn that a man known only as Mr. _____ wants to marry Nettie. Mr. _____ has a lover named Shug Avery, a sultry lounge singer whose photograph fascinates Celie. Alphonso refuses to let Nettie marry, and instead offers Mr. _____ the "ugly" Celie as a bride. Mr. _____ eventually accepts the offer, and takes Celie into a difficult and joyless married life. Nettie runs away from Alphonso and takes refuge at Celie's house. Mr. _____ still desires Nettie, and when he advances on her she flees for her own safety. Never hearing from Nettie again, Celie assumes she is dead.

Mr. _____'s sister Kate feels sorry for Celie, and tells her to fight back against Mr. _____ rather than submit to his abuses. Harpo, Mr. _____'s son, falls in love with a large, spunky girl named Sofia. Shug Avery comes to town to sing at a local bar, but Celie is not allowed to go see her. Sofia becomes pregnant and marries Harpo. Celie is amazed by Sofia's defiance in the face of Harpo's and Mr. _____'s attempts to treat Sofia as an inferior. Harpo's attempts to beat Sofia into submission consistently fail, as Sofia is by far the physically stronger of the two.

Shug falls ill and Mr. _____ takes her into his house. Shug is initially rude to Celie, but the two women become friends as Celie takes charge of nursing Shug. Celie finds herself infatuated with Shug and attracted to her sexually. Frustrated with Harpo's consistent attempts to subordinate her, Sofia moves out, taking her children. Several months later, Harpo opens a juke joint where Shug sings nightly. Celie grows confused over her feelings toward Shug.

Shug decides to stay when she learns that Mr. _____ beats Celie when Shug is away. Shug and Celie's relationship grows intimate,

3

and Shug begins to ask Celie questions about sex. Sofia returns for a visit and promptly gets in a fight with Harpo's new girlfriend, Squeak. In town one day, the mayor's wife, Miss Millie, asks Sofia to work as her maid. Sofia answers with a sassy "Hell no." When the mayor slaps Sofia for her insubordination, she returns the blow, knocking the mayor down. Sofia is sent to jail. Squeak's attempts to get Sofia freed are futile. Sofia is sentenced to work for twelve years as the mayor's maid.

Shug returns with a new husband, Grady. Despite her marriage, Shug instigates a sexual relationship with Celie, and the two frequently share the same bed. One night Shug asks Celie about her sister. Celie assumes Nettie is dead because she had promised to write to Celie but never did. Shug says she has seen Mr. _____ hide away numerous mysterious letters that have arrived in the mail. Shug manages to get her hands on one of these letters, and they find it is from Nettie. Searching through Mr. _____'s trunk, Celie and Shug find dozens of letters that Nettie has sent to Celie over the years. Overcome with emotion, Celie reads the letters in order, wondering how to keep herself from killing Mr. _____.

The letters indicate that Nettie befriended a missionary couple, Samuel and Corrine, and traveled with them to Africa to do ministry work. Samuel and Corrine have two adopted children, Olivia and Adam. Nettie and Corrine become close friends, but Corrine, noticing that her adopted children resemble Nettie, wonders if Nettie and Samuel have a secret past. Increasingly suspicious, Corrine tries to limit Nettie's role within her family.

Nettie becomes disillusioned with her missionary experience, as she finds the Africans self-centered and obstinate. Corrine becomes ill with a fever. Nettie asks Samuel to tell her how he adopted Olivia and Adam. Based on Samuel's story, Nettie realizes that the two children are actually Celie's biological children, alive after all. Nettie also learns that Alphonso is really only Nettie and Celie's step-father, not their real father. Their real father was a storeowner whom white men lynched because they resented his success. Alphonso told Celie and Nettie he was their real father because he wanted to inherit the house and property that was once their mother's.

Nettie confesses to Samuel and Corrine that she is in fact their children's biological aunt. The gravely ill Corrine refuses to believe Nettie. Corrine dies, but accepts Nettie's story and feels reconciled just before her death. Meanwhile, Celie visits Alphonso, who confirms Nettie's story, admitting that he is only the women's step-

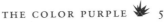

father. Celie begins to lose some of her faith in God, but Shug tries to get her to reimagine God in her own way, rather than in the traditional image of the old, bearded white man.

The mayor releases Sofia from her servitude six months early. At dinner one night, Celie finally releases her pent-up rage, angrily cursing Mr. _____ for his years of abuse. Shug announces that she and Celie are moving to Tennessee, and Squeak decides to go with them. In Tennessee, Celie spends her time designing and sewing individually tailored pairs of pants, eventually turning her hobby into a business. Celie returns to Georgia for a visit, and finds that Mr. _____ has reformed his ways and that Alphonso has died. Alphonso's house and land are now hers, so she moves there.

Meanwhile, Nettie and Samuel marry and prepare to return to America. Before they leave, Samuel's son, Adam, marries Tashi, a native African girl. Following African tradition, Tashi undergoes the painful rituals of female circumcision and facial scarring. In solidarity, Adam undergoes the same facial scarring ritual.

Celie and Mr. _____ reconcile and begin to genuinely enjoy each other's company. Now independent financially, spiritually, and emotionally, Celie is no longer bothered by Shug's passing flings with younger men. Sofia remarries Harpo and now works in Celie's clothing store. Nettie finally returns to America with Samuel and the children. Emotionally drained but exhilarated by the reunion with her sister, Celie notes that though she and Nettie are now old, she has never in her life felt younger.

CHARACTER LIST

Celie The protagonist and narrator of *The Color Purple*. Celie is a poor, uneducated black woman with a sad personal history. She survives a stepfather who rapes her and steals her babies and also survives an abusive husband. As an adult, Celie befriends and finds intimacy with a blues singer, Shug Avery, who gradually helps Celie find her voice. By the end of the novel, Celie is a happy, independent, and self-confident woman.

Nettie Celie's younger sister, whom Mr. _____ initially wanted to marry. Nettie runs from Alphonso to Mr. _____, and later runs away from Mr. _____. She meets a husband-and-wife pair of missionaries, Samuel and Corrine. With them, she moves to Africa to preach. Nettie becomes the caretaker of Samuel and Corrine's adopted children (who, Nettie later learns, are Celie's biological children, whom Celie and Nettie's stepfather stole and subsequently sold) and faithfully writes letters to Celie for decades. Nettie's experiences in Africa broaden the novel's scope, introducing issues of imperialism and pan-African struggles.

Mr. _____ Celie's husband, who abuses her for years. Mr. _____, whose first name is Albert, pines away for Shug during his marriage to Celie and hides Nettie's letters to Celie in his trunk for decades. After Celie finally defies Mr. _____, denouncing him for his abuse, he undergoes a deep personal transformation, reassessing his life and eventually becoming friends with Celie.

Shug Avery A sultry blues singer who first appears as Mr. _____'s mistress. Shug becomes Celie's friend and eventually her lover, all the while remaining a gentle mentor who helps Celie evolve into an independent and assertive woman. Shug does not at first appear to be the mothering kind, yet she nurtures Celie physically, spiritually, and emotionally. Shug gives Celie the idea of sewing pants for a living.

Harpo Mr. _____'s eldest son. Many of Harpo's actions overturn stereotypical gender roles. He confesses to Celie about his love for Sofia, cries in her arms, enjoys cooking and housework, kisses his children, and marries an independent woman, Sofia. However, Mr. _____'s expectations of stereotypical male dominance convince Harpo that he needs to beat Sofia. His efforts at abusing Sofia fail, since she is much stronger than he is. At the end of the novel, Harpo reforms his ways, and he and Sofia reconcile and save their marriage.

Sofia A large, fiercely independent woman who befriends Celie and marries Harpo. Sofia refuses to submit to whites, men, or anyone else who tries to dominate her. After defying the town's mayor, Sophia is sentenced to twelve years in jail, but the sentence is later commuted to twelve years labor as the mayor's maid. The hardship Sofia endures serves as a reminder of the costs of resistance and the difficulties of combating cultural and institutional racism.

Squeak Harpo's lover after Sofia leaves him. As a mulatto, a person of mixed black and white ancestry, Squeak highlights the complex nature of racial identification. Although abused like many of the women in the novel, Squeak eventually undergoes a transformation much like Celie's. She demands to be called by her real name, Mary Agnes, and she pursues a singing career.

Alphonso Celie and Nettie's stepfather, who the sisters think is their real father until Nettie learns the truth years later. When Celie is young, Alphonso rapes and abuses her until she moves out of the house. Unlike Mr. _____ and Harpo, who are transformed, Alphonso remains an abuser until his death. Celie inherits her house and property after Alphonso dies.

Samuel	A minister who, along with his wife, Corrine, adopts Celie's biological children, Olivia and Adam. A wise, spiritually mature black intellectual committed to "the uplift of black people everywhere," Samuel takes Corrine, Nettie, and the children to Africa for missionary work. He tells Nettie the story that makes her realize Alphonso is her stepfather rather than her biological father. After Corrine's death, Samuel marries Nettie.
Corrine	Samuel's wife. After moving to Africa, Corrine grows increasingly suspicious and jealous of Nettie's role in her family, convinced that Nettie and Samuel have had an affair. While still in Africa, Corrine dies from a fever, opening the opportunity for Nettie and Samuel to marry.
Olivia	Celie and Alphonso's biological daughter, who is adopted by Samuel and Corrine. Olivia develops a close sisterly relationship with Tashi, an Olinka village girl. This friendship, which crosses cultural boundaries, serves as an example of the strength of relationships between women.
Adam	Celie and Alphonso's biological son, who, like Olivia, is adopted by Samuel and Corrine. Adam falls in love with Tashi, a young Olinka girl. By marrying Tashi, Adam symbolically bridges Africa and America, and his respect for and deference to her subverts patriarchal notions that women are subordinate to men.
Tashi	An Olinka village girl who befriends Olivia and marries Adam. Tashi defies white imperialist culture and embodies the struggle of traditional cultural values against colonization. She chooses to undergo two painful African traditions—facial scarring and genital mutilation—as a way to physically differentiate her culture from imperialist culture.

CHARACTER LIST

Miss Millie The wife of the mayor of the town where Celie lives. Miss Millie is racist and condescending, but she admires the cleanliness and good manners of Sofia's children, so she asks Sofia to be her maid. Sofia replies, "Hell no," and is sent first to jail, then to Miss Millie's, where she ends up working as her maid after all.

Eleanor Jane The mayor's daughter. Eleanor Jane develops a strong attachment to Sofia and turns to her for emotional support. However, Sofia does not reciprocate Eleanor Jane's feelings because of the years of mistreatment she suffered at the hands of Eleanor Jane's parents. Toward the end of the novel, Eleanor Jane finally begins to understand the injustices Sofia and other blacks have suffered. She attempts to atone for her part in the unjust treatment of Sofia by caring for Sofia's daughter Henrietta.

Grady Shug's husband. Grady is a loving and sweet man, but also a womanizer. He spends Shug's money flamboyantly and frequently smokes marijuana. When Grady and Squeak begin an affair, Shug seems relieved to be rid of any responsibility to her relationship with Grady.

Kate One of Mr. _____'s sisters. Kate urges Celie to stand up for herself and defy Mr. _____'s abuses.

Analysis of Major Characters

Celie

As a young girl, Celie is constantly subjected to abuse and told she is ugly. She decides therefore that she can best ensure her survival by making herself silent and invisible. Celie's letters to God are her only outlet and means of self-expression. To Celie, God is a distant figure, who she doubts cares about her concerns.

Celie does little to fight back against her stepfather, Alphonso. Later in life, when her husband, Mr. _____, abuses her, she reacts in a similarly passive manner. However, Celie latches on to Shug Avery, a beautiful and seemingly empowered woman, as a role model. After Shug moves into Celie and Mr. _____'s home, Celie has the opportunity to befriend the woman whom she loves and to learn, at last, how to fight back.

Shug's maternal prodding helps spur Celie's development. Gradually, Celie recovers her own history, sexuality, spirituality, and voice. When Shug says Celie is "still a virgin" because she has never had a satisfying sex life, Shug demonstrates to Celie the renewing and empowering capacity of storytelling. Shug also opens Celie's eyes to new ideas about religion, empowering Celie to believe in a nontraditional, non-patriarchal version of God.

Nettie's long-lost letters, which Celie discovers with Shug's help hidden in Mr. _____'s trunk, fortify Celie's sense of self by informing her of her personal history and of the fate of her children. As her letters show, Celie gradually gains the ability to synthesize her thoughts and feelings into a voice that is fully her own. Celie's process of finding her own voice culminates with her enraged explosion at Mr. _____, in which she curses him for his years of abuse and abasement. Mr. _____ responds in his characteristic insulting manner, but his put-downs have no power once Celie possesses the sense of self-worth she previously lacked.

The self-actualization Celie achieves transforms her into a happy, successful, independent woman. Celie takes the act of sewing, which is traditionally thought of as a mere chore for women who are confined to a domestic role, and turns it into an outlet for creative self-expression and a profitable business. After being voiceless for so many years, she is finally content, fulfilled, and self-sufficient. When Nettie, Olivia, and Adam return to Georgia from Africa, Celie's circle of friends and family is finally reunited. Though Celie has endured many years of hardship, she says, "[D]on't think us feel old at all. . . . Matter of fact, I think this the youngest us ever felt."

SHUG AVERY

Our first impression of Shug is negative. We learn she has a reputation as a woman of dubious morals who dresses scantily, has some sort of "nasty woman disease," and is spurned by her own parents. Celie immediately sees something more in Shug. When Celie looks at Shug's photograph, not only does Shug's glamorous appearance amaze her, but Shug also reminds Celie of her "mama." Celie compares Shug to her mother throughout the novel. Unlike Celie's natural mother, who was oppressed by traditional gender roles, Shug refuses to allow herself to be dominated by anyone. Shug has fashioned her identity from her many experiences, instead of subjecting her will to others and allowing them to impose an identity upon her.

Though Shug's sexy style, sharp tongue, and many worldly experiences make her appear jaded, Shug is actually warm and compassionate at heart. When Shug falls ill, she not only appreciates, but also reciprocates the care and attention Celie lavishes upon her. As Shug's relationship with Celie develops, Shug fills the roles of mother, confidant, lover, sister, teacher, and friend. Shug's many roles make her an unpredictable and dynamic character who moves through a whirlwind of different cities, trysts, and late-night blues clubs. Despite her unpredictable nature and shifting roles, Shug remains Celie's most constant friend and companion throughout the novel.

MR. _____

Although Mr. _____'s development is not the subject of the novel, he undergoes just as significant a transformation as Celie does. Mr. _____ initially treats Celie as no more than an object. He beats her like an animal and shows no human connection, even during sex. He also hides Nettie's letters to Celie from Celie for years.

Mr. _____'s harsh treatment of Celie spurs her development. Celie's discovery of Nettie's letters begins her first experience with raw anger, which culminates in her angry denunciation of Mr. _____ in front of the others at dinner. Celie's newfound confidence, instilled in her by Shug, inspires her to react assertively and forcefully to Mr. _____'s abuse.

When Celie returns from Tennessee, she finds that Mr. _____ has reevaluated his life and attempted to correct his earlier wrongs. Mr. _____ finally listens to Celie, and the two come to enjoy conversing and sewing together. Mr. _____ eventually expresses his wish to have an equal and mutually respectful marriage with Celie, but she declines.

NETTIE

Though younger than her sister, Nettie often acts as Celie's protector. Nettie is highly intellectual and from an early age recognizes the value of education. However, even though Nettie is smart and ambitious, Mr. _____ effectively silences her by secretly hiding her letters from Celie. In her letters to Celie, Nettie writes that she is lonely, showing that like Celie, Nettie needs a sympathetic audience to listen to her thoughts and concerns.

Critics have faulted Nettie's letters for being digressive and boring in comparison to Celie's. Although Nettie's letters are indeed quite encyclopedic and contain less raw experience and emotion, they play an important role in the novel. As a black intellectual traveling the world in pursuit of "the uplift of black people everywhere," Nettie has a vastly different experience from Celie. Yet her letters, which recount the problems Nettie encounters in Africa, broaden the novel's scope and show that oppression—of women by men, of blacks by whites, and even of blacks by blacks—is universal. The imperial, racial, and cultural conflict and oppression Nettie encounters in Africa parallel the smaller-scale abuses and hardships that Celie experiences in Georgia.

THEMES, MOTIFS & SYMBOLS

THEMES

Themes are the fundamental and often universal ideas explored in a literary work.

THE POWER OF NARRATIVE AND VOICE

Walker emphasizes throughout the novel that the ability to express one's thoughts and feelings is crucial to developing a sense of self. Initially, Celie is completely unable to resist those who abuse her. Remembering Alphonso's warning that she "better not never tell nobody but God" about his abuse of her, Celie feels that the only way to persevere is to remain silent and invisible. Celie is essentially an object, an entirely passive party who has no power to assert herself through action or words. Her letters to God, in which she begins to pour out her story, become her only outlet. However, because she is so unaccustomed to articulating her experience, her narrative is initially muddled despite her best efforts at transparency.

In Shug and Sofia, Celie finds sympathetic ears and learns lessons that enable her to find her voice. In renaming Celie a "virgin," Shug shows Celie that she can create her own narrative, a new interpretation of herself and her history that counters the interpretations forced upon her. Gradually Celie begins to flesh out more of her story by telling it to Shug. However, it is not until Celie and Shug discover Nettie's letters that Celie finally has enough knowledge of herself to form her own powerful narrative. Celie's forceful assertion of this newfound power, her cursing of Mr. _____ for his years of abuse, is the novel's climax. Celie's story dumbfounds and eventually humbles Mr. _____, causing him to reassess and change his own life.

Though Walker clearly wishes to emphasize the power of narrative and speech to assert selfhood and resist oppression, the novel acknowledges that such resistance can be risky. Sofia's forceful outburst in response to Miss Millie's invitation to be her maid costs her twelve years of her life. Sofia regains her freedom eventually, so she is not totally defeated, but she pays a high price for her words.

THE POWER OF STRONG FEMALE RELATIONSHIPS

Throughout *The Color Purple,* Walker portrays female friendships as a means for women to summon the courage to tell stories. In turn, these stories allow women to resist oppression and dominance. Relationships among women form a refuge, providing reciprocal love in a world filled with male violence.

Female ties take many forms: some are motherly or sisterly, some are in the form of mentor and pupil, some are sexual, and some are simply friendships. Sofia claims that her ability to fight comes from her strong relationships with her sisters. Nettie's relationship with Celie anchors her through years of living in the unfamiliar culture of Africa. Samuel notes that the strong relationships among Olinka women are the only thing that makes polygamy bearable for them. Most important, Celie's ties to Shug bring about Celie's gradual redemption and her attainment of a sense of self.

THE CYCLICAL NATURE OF RACISM AND SEXISM

Almost none of the abusers in Walker's novel are stereotypical, one-dimensional monsters whom we can dismiss as purely evil. Those who perpetuate violence are themselves victims, often of sexism, racism, or paternalism. Harpo, for example, beats Sofia only after his father implies that Sofia's resistance makes Harpo less of a man. Mr. _____ is violent and mistreats his family much like his own tyrantlike father treated him. Celie advises Harpo to beat Sofia because she is jealous of Sofia's strength and assertiveness.

The characters are largely aware of the cyclical nature of harmful behavior. For instance, Sofia tells Eleanor Jane that societal influence makes it almost inevitable that her baby boy will grow up to be a racist. Only by forcefully talking back to the men who abuse them and showing them a new way of doing things do the women of the novel break these cycles of sexism and violence, causing the men who abused them to stop and reexamine their ways.

THE DISRUPTION OF TRADITIONAL GENDER ROLES

Many characters in the novel break the boundaries of traditional male or female gender roles. Sofia's strength and sass, Shug's sexual assertiveness, and Harpo's insecurity are major examples of such disparity between a character's gender and the traits he or she displays. This blurring of gender traits and roles sometimes involves sexual ambiguity, as we see in the sexual relationship that develops between Celie and Shug.

Disruption of gender roles sometimes causes problems. Harpo's insecurity about his masculinity leads to marital problems and his attempts to beat Sofia. Likewise, Shug's confident sexuality and resistance to male domination cause her to be labeled a tramp. Throughout the novel, Walker wishes to emphasize that gender and sexuality are not as simple as we may believe. Her novel subverts and defies the traditional ways in which we understand women to be women and men to be men.

MOTIFS

Motifs are recurring structures, contrasts, or literary devices that can help to develop and inform the text's major themes.

LETTERS

Walker uses the novel's epistolary (letter-writing) form to emphasize the power of communication. Celie writes letters to God, and Nettie writes letters to Celie. Both sisters gain strength from their letter writing, but they are saved only when they receive responses to their letters. Therefore, although writing letters enables self-expression and confession, it requires a willing audience. When Celie never responds to Nettie's letters, Nettie feels lost because Celie is her only audience. Nettie grows disillusioned with her missionary work because the imperialists will not listen to her and because the Olinka villagers are stubborn. Only after Nettie returns home to Celie, an audience guaranteed to listen, does she feel fulfilled and freed.

THE RURAL FARM COMMUNITY

Walker sets most of her novel in a rural farm community that has few visitors, and she focuses on colorful portraits of each of her characters. By focusing on the personal lives and transformations of her characters, Walker renders public events almost irrelevant. When Shug and Celie hear news of current events from the outside world, it all just sounds "crazy" to them. The unspecific time and place broaden the novel's scope, making its themes more universal.

COLORS

Throughout the novel, the appearance of brighter colors indicates the liberation various characters experience. Walker uses color to signal renewals and rebirths at several points in the novel. When

Kate takes Celie shopping for a new dress, the only color options are drab ones—brown, maroon, and dark blue. Later, Celie and Sofia use bright yellow fabric from Shug's dress to make a quilt. When Celie describes her religious awakening, she marvels how she never noticed the wonders that God has made, such as "the color purple." Upon Mr. _____'s transformation, he paints the entire interior of his house "fresh and white," signaling his new beginning.

Symbols

> *Symbols are objects, characters, figures, or colors used to represent abstract ideas or concepts.*

Sewing and Quilts

In general, sewing in *The Color Purple* symbolizes the power women can gain from productively channeling their creative energy. After Sofia and Celie argue about the advice Celie has given Harpo, Sofia signals a truce by suggesting they make a quilt. The quilt, composed of diverse patterns sewn together, symbolizes diverse people coming together in unity. Like a patchwork quilt, the community of love that surrounds Celie at the end of the novel incorporates men and women who are bonded by family and friendship, and who have different gender roles, sexual orientations, and talents. Another important instance of sewing in the novel is Celie's pants-sewing business. With Shug's help, Celie overturns the idea that sewing is marginal and unimportant women's labor, and she turns it into a lucrative, empowering source of economic independence.

God

In the early parts of the novel, Celie sees God as her listener and helping hand, yet Celie does not have a clear understanding of who God is. She knows deep down that her image of God as a white patriarch "don't seem quite right," but she says it's all she has. Shug invites Celie to imagine God as something radically different, as an "it" that delights in creation and just wants human beings to love what it has created. Eventually, Celie stops thinking of God as she stops thinking of the other men in her life—she "git man off her eyeball" and tells God off, writing, "You must be sleep." But after Celie has chased her patriarchal God away and come up with a new concept of God, she writes in her last letter, "Dear God. Dear stars, dear trees, dear sky, dear peoples. Dear Everything. Dear God." This reimagining of God on her own terms symbolizes Celie's move from an object of someone else's care to an independent woman. It also indicates that her voice is now sufficiently empowered to create her own narrative.

Summary & Analysis

Letters 1–10

Summary

The Color Purple opens with Celie's memory of her father's command that she stay quiet about his abuse of her. The rest of the novel is composed of letters, and we begin with the first of many private letters Celie writes to God. In her first letter, Celie asks for guidance because she does not understand what is happening to her. Only fourteen, Celie is already pregnant with her second child—the result of rape and incest. Alphonso, Celie's father, has turned to Celie for sexual gratification because Celie's mother is ill and can no longer endure Alphonso's sexual demands.

Celie's mother dies. Celie writes that Alphonso stole Celie's first baby while she was sleeping and killed it in the woods, and she believes he will kill her second baby as well. However, Alphonso does not kill the second baby, and Celie suspects that he instead sold the child to a married couple. Celie is left with her breasts filled with milk for no one.

From Celie's fourth letter to God, we learn that Alphonso has brought home a new wife, though this marriage does not end the physical and sexual abuse Celie endures. Alphonso beats Celie for winking at a boy in church, though she may have just had something stuck in her eye. Later, he beats her again for dressing "trampy."

Celie and her younger sister, Nettie, learn that a man, to whom Celie refers only as Mr. _____, has shown an interest in marrying Nettie. The man is recently widowed because his first wife was murdered by her lover. Alphonso's new wife tells Celie and Nettie that Mr. _____ also had a lover outside of marriage, a woman named Shug Avery. The girls find a photograph of Shug, and her bright, glamorous face captivates Celie, who has never seen anyone like her.

Alphonso refuses to hand Nettie over to Mr. _____, stating that she is far too young and inexperienced to marry a man with children. Alphonso wants Nettie to continue her schooling and offers the man Celie instead. Alphonso claims that though Celie is ugly, a liar, and "spoiled twice," she is older and hardworking and owns her own cow, which she could bring into the marriage.

After brooding over the offer for a few months, Mr. ____ makes up his mind to take Celie. Celie desperately wants to stay in school, but Alphonso says she is too dumb to learn anything. Celie spends her wedding day bandaging a wound from a rock Mr. ____'s son throws at her, untangling her screaming stepdaughters' hair, and cooking dinner. Celie spends a joyless wedding night with Mr. ____ on top of her, all the while worrying about Nettie's safety.

While in town one day, Celie catches sight of a young girl who she thinks may be her lost daughter. The girl closely resembles Celie, especially her eyes. The little girl's mother talks kindly with Celie after she follows them into a fabric store, where Celie learns that the mother calls her daughter Olivia, the same name Celie gave her own daughter and embroidered on her diapers before the infant was taken away. In the store, the racist shopkeeper treats Olivia's mother poorly, making her buy thread she does not want and tearing off her new fabric without bothering to measure it.

Analysis

The epistolary, or letter-writing, form of *The Color Purple* resembles a diary, since Celie tells her story through private letters that she writes to God. Therefore, Celie narrates her life story with complete candor and honesty. As a poor African-American woman in rural Georgia in the 1930s and a victim of domestic abuse, Celie is almost completely voiceless and disenfranchised in everyday society. However, Celie's letters enable her to break privately the silence that is normally imposed upon her.

Celie's confessional narrative is reminiscent of African-American slave narratives from the nineteenth century. These early slave narratives, which took the form of song, dance, storytelling, and other arts, ruptured the silence imposed on the black community. Yet, unlike Celie's letters, these slave narratives employed codes, symbols, humor, and other methods to hide their true intent. Slaves took these measures to prevent slave owners from discovering the slaves' ability to communicate, articulate, and reflect on their unhappiness, but Celie takes no such protective measures.

Celie's letters, though completely candid and confessional, are sometimes difficult to decipher because Celie's ability to narrate her life story is highly limited. When Celie's cursing mother asks who fathered Celie's baby, Celie, remembering Alphonso's command to keep quiet, says the baby is God's because she does not know what else to say. Similarly, Celie does not know what to say about her mother's death, her abuse, or her stolen babies. Celie knows how to state the events plainly, but often does not know how to interpret them. Despite the abuses she endures, Celie has little consciousness of injustice and shows little or no anger.

Walker's use of Celie's own voice, however underdeveloped, allows Walker to tell the history of black women in the rural South in a sympathetic and realistic way. Unlike a historian's perspective, which can be antiseptic and overly analytical, Celie's letters offer a powerful first-person account of the institutions of racism and sexism. Celie's simple narrative brings us into her isolated world with language that reveals both pain and detached numbness: "My momma dead. She die screaming and cussing. She scream at me. She cuss at me."

Like her voice, Celie's faith is prominent but underdeveloped. Celie relies heavily on God as her listener and source of strength, but she sometimes blurs the distinction between God's authority and that of Alphonso. She confesses that God, rather than Alphonso, killed her baby, and she never makes any association between the injustice she experiences in her life and the ability of God to overturn or prevent this injustice.

LETTERS 11–21

SUMMARY

Nettie runs away from Alphonso and finds refuge with Celie and Mr. _____. It quickly becomes clear that Mr. _____ still has an eye for Nettie. Whenever Mr. _____ pays Nettie a compliment, she passes it on to Celie. However, Nettie refuses Mr. _____'s advances, and she is soon forced to leave. Never hearing from Nettie again, Celie presumes her sister is dead.

Mr. _____'s two sisters, Kate and Carrie, visit and treat Celie with kindness, complimenting her on her housekeeping and her care of the children. Kate tells her brother that Celie needs new clothes, and though he seems surprised to learn that Celie would have needs, he allows the purchase. Celie is so grateful for her new dress, she does not know how to thank Kate. Kate also demands that Mr. _____'s eldest son, Harpo, help Celie with chores. Harpo has refused to help because he considers chores a woman's job. Kate's demand angers her brother, and the two get in a heated fight. When Kate leaves the house, she tells Celie to fight back against Mr. _____, but Celie does not see what good fighting will do.

Harpo confides in Celie that he has fallen in love with a spunky, robust young girl named Sofia. Celie's thoughts linger on the sexy Shug Avery, who she learns is coming to town to sing at a local bar called the Lucky Star. Celie longs to go to the bar, merely to lay eyes on Shug. However, the only member of the household who sees Shug is Mr. _____, who spends the weekend with her. When he returns, Celie resists the temptation to ask Mr. _____ all the questions she has about Shug's dresses, her body, and her voice. Instead, Celie and Harpo toil silently through the extra work they are given while Mr. _____ is lovesick and depressed after Shug's departure. Harpo tries to complain to his father about the heavy workload, but Celie notes that Harpo is just as unskilled at arguing with Mr. _____ as she is.

Sofia's parents will not let her marry Harpo because of the legacy of his murdered mother, and Mr. _____ is also opposed to the idea. However, after Sofia gets pregnant, marriage becomes inevitable. Celie is struck by the vivaciousness and unflinching strength Sofia displays as she talks back to Harpo and Mr. _____, as defiance is foreign to her own relationships with the two men.

When Sofia and Harpo marry, Celie helps them fix up an old shack on Mr. _____'s land, which they use as a home. Sofia and Harpo are happy newlyweds and doting parents, and Sofia keeps up her spunky spirit, demanding that Harpo help with the chores and refusing to acquiesce to her husband or father-in-law. Frustrated, Harpo asks both Celie and Mr. _____ how to get Sofia to behave, and both give him the only advice they know: to beat her. However, Sofia is physically very strong, and Harpo's attempts to beat her typically result in more injury to himself than to his wife.

Celie worries that in advising Harpo to beat Sofia she has somehow committed a sin against Sofia's spirit, and she has trouble sleeping for more than a month. Sofia learns that it was Celie who advised Harpo to beat her, so she angrily confronts Celie. Celie confesses that she is jealous that Sofia knows how to defend herself and fight back against her husband. Sofia feels sorry for Celie's timidity and submissiveness, and the two make up and laugh about the incident. They talk about their families, and Sofia mentions she has six brothers. She also has five sisters, and all six girls are strong and "stick together." Now friends, Sofia and Celie decide to make quilt pieces out of the curtains that were torn during Sofia and Harpo's recent fights. Celie no longer has trouble sleeping.

ANALYSIS

In this section, Walker begins to develop the idea that people can attain power by strengthening their own voices. The Celie we have seen so far completely lacks power. She is essentially an object of others who is very passive in her interactions, especially those with men. However, Celie shows she is aware that others see her as a powerless object when she tells Sofia she is jealous of her assertive, self-defensive personality. When Kate tells Mr. _____ that Celie needs new clothes, Celie is acutely aware that Mr. _____ thinks of her as little more than dirt, saying that when he looks at her, it's like he's looking at the earth, trying to determine if it needs anything.

Initially, Celie's advice that Harpo beat Sofia seems out of character, but we see that it is a result of the cyclical nature of abuse and oppression. When Harpo asks Celie for advice, Celie is given a rare opportunity to participate in the control and abuse of a woman other than herself. In her weakness and pain, Celie seizes this opportunity, but she quickly realizes that it represents a "sin against Sofia spirit." Celie interprets her own act with surprising sophistication, realizing and admitting to Sofia that she gave the advice because she is jealous that Sofia knows how to fight back against abuse.

Sofia's comment to Celie that she has tight-knit relationships with her five strong sisters implies that deep ties among women are a powerful means to combat sexism and abuse. Celie first witnesses Sofia's assertiveness and autonomy when Sofia meets Mr. _____ and defies his attempts to control her. Sofia denies Mr. _____'s accusation that she is in trouble and therefore will end up on the streets. Sofia refuses to despair at her own pregnancy and rebuffs Mr. _____'s attempts to make her miserable. Likewise, Sofia's refusal to stop talking when Mr. _____ or Harpo enters the room demonstrates that she does not view her identity as a woman simply in terms of reliance on and subjugation to men. Sofia's defiance of the customs of patriarchy amazes Celie.

Walker argues that mastering one's own story and finding someone to listen and respond to it are crucial steps toward self-empowerment and autonomy.

Celie's lack of voice becomes more obvious in this section, as Nettie observes that seeing Celie with Mr. _____ and his children is like "seeing [Celie] buried." Nettie is the first of several women who tell Celie to fight back. Celie's explanation to Kate that she does not want to fight because it is too risky seems fatalistic and self-defeating, but Celie is right—there are significant, possibly even fatal, dangers inherent in resistance. Walker explores this tension between safety and danger throughout the novel.

Celie is also reluctant to resist because she lacks the tools she needs to fight back successfully—namely, a sense of self and an ability to create and express her own story. Nettie tries to help build Celie's sense of self by passing along to Celie Mr. _____'s compliments, which Celie admits bolster her self-image. Soon after, Celie begins her first efforts at self-expression when she tries to thank Kate for buying her a new dress. She becomes frustrated and flushed, unable to find the words. When Kate tells Celie not to worry and that she deserves more, Celie thinks, "Maybe so." Celie's strained attempt to communicate her own feelings and her admission that she feels she deserves more than she has are important first steps in Celie's process of empowerment. At the same time, Celie's inability to convey her feelings of gratitude to Kate, a sympathetic audience, demonstrates the depth of Celie's lack of self-understanding.

Celie has difficulty defining, interpreting and speaking about her self because, as she confesses to God, she has grown so numb in the face of adversity. She admits that, to get by, she pretends she is a tree. Rather than react emotionally or intellectually to adversity, Celie has found it easier and less dangerous to become wooden—to remain stone-faced and unthinking rather than attempt to reflect, interpret, or narrate.

LETTERS 22–33

SUMMARY

Shug Avery is sick, likely due to a sexually transmitted disease, and no one in the town will take her in. Both her mother and father say that Shug's promiscuity has gotten her what she deserves. Mr. _____ leaves home unannounced and returns with the feeble Shug in his wagon. Though weak, feverish, and malnourished, Shug still has a razor-sharp tongue. Her first words to Celie upon meeting her are, "You sure is ugly." Despite Shug's nasty demeanor, Celie grows increasingly mesmerized by the sexy singer, whose stylish dresses, makeup, and slender figure are unlike anything Celie has ever seen. When Celie sees Shug unclothed for the first time, she confesses that she feels a sexual attraction.

Shug's condition improves due to Celie's care, and the two become friends. Shug's improved disposition does not change the disdainful way she treats Mr. _____, whose first name, we learn from Shug, is Albert. Shug constantly teases Mr. _____ and calls him weak for not standing up to his own father, but he nonetheless remains love-struck. Harpo has been eating like a horse and has gained such a potbelly that the others laugh and ask when his baby is due. Harpo later confesses to Celie that he has been eating so much in an attempt to get as big as Sofia so that he can finally beat her into submission. This time, Celie advises against beating Sofia, telling Harpo that his relationship with his wife is one of genuine mutual love and should not be compared to the callous, loveless marriage between Celie and Mr. _____.

Mr. _____'s father and his brother, Tobias, come to visit. Both men disapprove of Shug staying at the house. Celie overhears Mr. _____'s father criticizing Shug's promiscuity, so she secretly spits in his drinking water. When Mr. _____'s father reprimands his son for his lifestyle, Celie and Mr. _____ share a moment of eye contact that Celie describes as "the closest us ever felt."

Sofia confesses to Celie that she is sad because, ever since Harpo has been eating and brooding, the two have lost the sexual vitality that was once a central part of their marriage. Sofia is angry with Harpo for his insistence on trying to take away her independence and assertiveness. Eventually, Sofia decides to move in with her sister, taking her children with her. Harpo tries to hide his feelings when Sofia leaves, but Celie sees him wipe away a tear with his baby's cloth diaper.

Once Sofia has been gone for six months, Harpo and a friend open a juke joint on their land. By hiring Shug to sing there, they draw a crowd to the place. Shug persuades Mr. _____ to allow Celie to go watch her sing. Celie sits with Mr. _____ and admires Shug onstage. She feels confused, sad, and alone when she notices the special eye contact that goes on between Mr. _____ and Shug. Celie's spirits lift when she hears Shug call out her name and dedicate a song to her, as this is the first time anyone has ever named anything after Celie. Celie knows that it is right for Mr. _____ and Shug to love each other, but she is confused over the pangs in her own heart and her increasing lovesickness for Shug.

ANALYSIS

Here, as in the previous section, Celie cannot match what she feels with what she says. When Shug arrives and needs care, Celie feels ecstatic, but she says nothing because she does not know anything and because she feels it is not her place to speak. Celie has been silenced for so long that she has become accustomed to having no voice. Her natural reaction is to say nothing.

However, Celie begins to understand that her perception of herself differs from the way others perceive her. Reflecting on herself and on her lot, Celie writes, "I might as well be under the table, for all they care. I hate the way I look, I hate the way I'm dress." These beginnings of self-awareness represent a foundational first step toward Celie's empowerment.

As her sense of self develops, Celie begins to perceive weakness and shortcomings in the men who oppress her. She also begins to react in an assertive manner. Looking at Mr. _____, Celie critically notes that he has a weak chin and wears dirty clothes. Angry at Mr. _____'s father for his unkind words about Shug, Celie retaliates secretly but assertively, spitting in the old man's drinking water and threatening to put Shug's pee in his glass the next time he visits. Celie also displays assertiveness when Harpo again asks for her advice about Sofia. This time, Celie finds words to express her true feelings, and she tells Harpo that abusing Sofia is not the answer.

Walker's idea of the varied, multilayered nature of intimacy among women also emerges in Celie and Shug's relationship. Walker understands sexuality and sexual orientation as a spectrum of possibilities rather than as two, polar-opposite choices. Thus, like race, sexuality can be difficult to define, and more complex than the simple dichotomy of heterosexuality and homosexuality. Celie's feelings toward Shug are sexual, but they are also based on friendship, gratitude, camaraderie, and admiration. Celie does feel sexually aroused when she sees Shug naked, but just as important are the feelings of maternal tenderness toward Shug that Celie confesses to God when describing how she nurses Shug back to health.

LETTERS 34–43

SUMMARY

*Harpo say, I love you, Squeak. He kneel down and try
to put his arms round her waist. She stand up. My
name Mary Agnes, she say.* (See QUOTATIONS, p. 45)

Celie is upset that Shug is soon leaving the house. Longing for
Shug to stay, Celie tells Shug that Mr. ＿＿＿ beats her when Shug is
away. When Shug asks why he beats her, Celie answers, "For
being me and not you." Shug kisses Celie on the shoulder and
declares she will not leave until she knows Mr. ＿＿＿ would not
even think about beating Celie.

Shug and Celie's relationship grows increasingly intimate, and
Shug coaxes Celie to talk about sex for the first time. Celie's words,
not surprisingly, are dismal. She says she despises sex and that during the act she typically pretends she is not even there. Shug tells
Celie that, in her mind, Celie is still a virgin. To Shug, a woman's real
loss of virginity is not her first sex act, but the first time she experiences the pleasure of an orgasm. Celie finds the idea of pleasure
sexy, otherworldly, and shocking.

Shug makes Celie take a mirror and look closely at her own sexual organs for the first time in her life. They act like little girls, gig-
gling and worrying about getting caught. When Celie gets her first
long, bold look at herself "down there," she is not disgusted by
what she sees, but states plainly that it is hers. Celie tells Shug that
she does not care if Shug sleeps with Mr. ＿＿＿, but later when she
hears them together Celie cries.

Shug continues to sing at Harpo's juke joint, to increasingly large
crowds. Sofia makes a surprise visit one night, looking healthy and
happy with a new boyfriend in her arms. Sofia and Harpo dance and
make conversation, infuriating Harpo's new girlfriend, Squeak, a
young mixed-race woman who does anything Harpo says. Not
knowing the trouble she is getting herself into, Squeak calls Sofia a
bitch and slaps her across the face. Sofia promptly knocks out two
of Squeak's teeth, and coolly departs with her new man.

Sofia's boldness soon gets her in trouble. When the mayor's wife,
Miss Millie, notices the cleanliness of Sofia's children and asks Sofia
to be her maid, Sofia responds with a curt "Hell no." The mayor
slaps Sofia for her sass, and Sofia knocks him down, an offense that

lands her in jail. Upon visiting, Celie finds Sofia badly beaten, and her ribs and skull cracked. Celie is scared, but sits down and grooms Sofia. At home, everyone decides they need to get Sofia out of jail. Squeak admits that she is the niece of the white prison warden, so Mr. _____ tells her to go plead for Sofia's release. Celie and the others dress Squeak up "like she a white woman" and send her off, armed with fraudulent words to trick the warden into granting Sofia's release.

The warden does not release Sofia and instead brutally rapes Squeak, who comes home limping, her dress in tatters. Devastated, she tells the others what happened. She demands that Harpo call her by her real name, Mary Agnes. Sofia, rather than being released from prison, is sentenced to work as a maid for the mayor's wife. Squeak helps Sofia with the mayor's children, and begins to sing—first Shug's songs, then songs she makes up herself.

ANALYSIS

Continuing the trend seen in her previous letters, Celie begins to take more pronounced steps in interpreting herself and the world around her. When Celie tells Shug that Mr. _____ beats her "[f]or being me and not you," she demonstrates that her self-analysis is becoming increasingly developed and sophisticated.

One reason for Celie's increased self-awareness is the sexual awakening that she experiences through Shug's education. Shug declares Celie a virgin and renames her Miss Celie, giving Celie a new identity in both a figurative and a literal sense. Shug's pronouncement of Celie as a virgin and the new name Shug gives Celie are critical to Celie's empowerment to tell her own story and to her sense of self.

Shug's renaming of Celie flies in the face of traditional definitions of virginity. Shug redefines virginity in her own terms, saying it is not lost when a man penetrates a woman but rather when a woman chooses to have sex and finds it physically and emotionally pleasurable. By redefining virginity in her own terms, Shug encourages Celie to take similar control over her own situation by interpreting it in a new way. The fact that Shug can suddenly term a married woman with two children a virgin introduces the possibility that there is a submerged, untold story in Celie's life. Shug helps Celie realize that there are alternatives to the mainstream ways of thinking, perceiving, interpreting, and behaving that the dominant members of society impose upon her. Recognizing the existence of these alternatives gives Celie a sense of control and is an important step in her move toward independence.

Yet Sofia's punishment makes it clear that challenging and reinterpreting mainstream perspectives often comes at a price. Sofia, who is robust and healthy and has a loving family and a comfortable material existence, is vastly different from white society's stereotype of the subservient black woman. Sofia bluntly asserts her unwillingness to conform to this stereotype by answering Miss Millie's employment offer with a resounding "Hell no." However, this resistance costs Sofia a cracked skull, broken ribs, a body covered with bruises, and twelve years of her life. Likewise, when Squeak resists by venturing forth in an attempt to free Sofia from prison, she is raped. It is clear that although Walker views resistance as crucial, she does not want to romanticize it as an act free of pain or consequences.

Ultimately, neither Sofia's nor Squeak's misfortunes defeat them. For Walker, the most basic indication of victory is the ability to tell one's story, and neither Sofia nor Squeak loses her voice. Sofia maintains her resistance even when pressed into service as Miss Millie's maid. Likewise, when Harpo tries to tell the others the story of Squeak's rape, Squeak interrupts him, telling him to be quiet because she wants to tell her own story. Additionally, in the same way Shug renames Celie a virgin, Squeak renames herself to Harpo, rejecting the diminutive nickname he has given her in favor of her real name, Mary Agnes. Just as Celie's renaming is enabling her to reinterpret the world, Squeak's renaming opens up the gifts that have long been hidden inside her, and she starts to sing.

LETTERS 44–60

SUMMARY

Us sleep like sisters, me and Shug.
(See QUOTATIONS, p. 46)

Sofia complains that the mayor's family is backward. To illustrate its backwardness, she tells a story: Miss Millie pestered her husband into buying her a car, but he refused to teach her to drive. Miss Millie finally asked Sofia to teach her to drive, which she did, with some success. As a Christmas reward, Miss Millie said she would drive

Sofia to see her children, whom she had not seen in five years. Miss Millie said Sofia could visit the children for an entire day. However, only a few minutes into the visit, Miss Millie tried to drive back into town but got stuck in the driveway because she did not know how to operate the car in reverse. Frustrated that she had stripped the car's gears, Miss Millie refused to allow Sofia's brother-in-law to drive her into town, saying she could never ride in a car "with a strange colored man." Miss Millie demanded that Sofia drive her home, even though Sofia had been able to spend only fifteen minutes with her children. Whenever Sofia mentions this incident, Miss Millie calls her "ungrateful."

Shug writes that she has a big surprise, which turns out to be a new husband, Grady. Grady rubs Celie the wrong way, as he makes a flamboyant display of spending Shug's money. Celie and Mr. _____ feel left out, as the love of their lives has returned home with another man. During Christmas, Grady and Mr. _____ drink while Shug and Celie spend time together. Shug's singing career has grown rapidly, and she knows many famous musicians. Shug asks whether sex is going any better between Celie and Mr. _____, and Celie says it has not improved much, so she thinks she is still a virgin. Shug sleeps in Celie's bed, where the two return to sisterly conversations about sex. Celie finally tells Shug her entire life story. It is the first time Celie tells about the rape by her stepfather, her silence, her pregnancies, and Nettie's disappearance. When Celie finishes her story, tears flow, and Shug says that she loves Celie. Their conversation, kisses, and intimacy turn highly sexual.

One night in bed Shug asks Celie to tell her more about Nettie because—aside from Shug—Nettie is the only person Celie has every really loved. Celie says she fears Nettie is dead because she has not received any letters from her. Shug mentions that she often sees Mr. _____ taking mysterious letters from the mailbox and hiding them in his coat pocket. A week later, Shug recovers the most recent of these letters, which has stamps from Africa on it. The letter is from Nettie. Nettie says she is alive and well and that she has been sending letters all along. Knowing Mr. _____, she assumes Celie has received none of them.

Celie realizes that Mr. _____ must be keeping all Nettie's letters in his locked trunk. Shug gets the key, and the two women open the trunk one night when they are home alone. Inside, they find dozens of letters from Nettie, some opened, some still sealed. Shug and Celie steam open the sealed letters and replace the empty envelopes in the trunk. Shug helps Celie put the letters in chronological order. Crying and struggling over unfamiliar words, Celie reads only the first seven letters before Grady and Mr. _____ return.

Celie reads that when Nettie first left Mr. _____'s house years ago, he followed her and tried to rape her. When Nettie fought back, Mr. _____ cursed her, saying that she would never again hear from Celie. It turns out that the woman whom Celie saw in the fabric store years ago, whose daughter looked just like Celie's daughter, is named Corrine. Nettie became friends with Corrine and her husband, Samuel, who were members of a Christian ministry planning to travel to Africa for missionary work. Nettie developed a huge appetite for learning, and after reading all of Samuel and Corrine's books about African history, decided to accompany them to Africa to help them start their missionary school. Nettie also learned that Samuel and Corrine's children, Olivia and Adam, are, in fact, Celie's lost children. Nettie traveled to New York and marveled at black society in Harlem, where liberated blacks own wealthy-looking houses. Nettie then crossed the Atlantic by boat, stopping first in Senegal, then Liberia, and finally a small village where she is doing missionary work. Nettie writes that she is amazed by the richness of African culture and the darkness of the native Africans' skin.

Celie is nearly blinded with rage when it sinks in that Mr. _____ has been hiding Nettie's letters from her. She feels sick and numb and has an overwhelming desire to kill Mr. _____. Trying to keep the peace, Shug tells Celie lengthy stories about her past with Mr. _____, who had once been a fun, sexy young man who made Shug very happy. But Celie remains in her own world, unafraid of Mr. _____ and even numb to Shug.

ANALYSIS

By listening to Celie's story, Shug enables Celie to open up emotionally. When Celie finally articulates the hardships she has endured, she no longer reacts like "wood," instead crying tears when she realizes the sadness of her own narrative. However, though Celie's newfound life story is a sad one, it is also a hopeful one because of her growing sexual and emotional relationship with Shug. Celie's sense of self has developed as a result of watching and learning from Shug. Shug serves as a model for Celie, a woman who embodies everything Celie lacks. At the same time, Shug is also a kind of double. In Shug's sad eyes, Celie sees the image of her own suffering. Gradually,

Celie's and Shug's impact on each other becomes reciprocal. They have even begun to take on each other's attributes. Celie's love and care have softened Shug's heart and made her more gentle and nurturing, while Celie has become more sexually vibrant and assertive.

This relationship between Celie and Shug is centered around the idea of storytelling. Numerous times, Celie mentions how much she and Shug talk to each other. Their constant communication is a giant step away from Celie's earlier silence. Nettie's letters also symbolize a narrative that has been suppressed by silence. In finding and reading the letters, Celie in effect resurrects Nettie's buried voice and begins to feel independent. However, only with Shug's help can Celie discover Nettie's story, put it in order, and decipher the parts of it she cannot understand herself. Learning that Nettie is alive gives Celie the strength necessary for self-reliance, and she ceases to fear Mr. _____ or rely as heavily on Shug.

Nettie's letters also place Celie's story within a much larger context. Until now, the plot of *The Color Purple* has been confined to a small set of people in a small town in rural Georgia. This insulation and isolation contrasts sharply with Nettie's experience, which has brought her to a village in Africa. Celie remarks that Nettie's letters are covered with stamps that have the picture of the Queen of England on them, signaling that blacks in Africa are also oppressed and dominated. The images in Nettie's letters not only open Celie's eyes to the outside world, but also link the personal oppression Celie has felt with the broader themes of domination and exploitation on the continent of Africa.

Another important element of Nettie's experience is her exposure to free blacks who are prospering in the North, namely in the Harlem neighborhood of New York. The idea of economically successful and independent blacks is largely foreign to Southern black women like Nettie and Celie, who are accustomed only to denigration, denial, and subservience at the hands of both whites and black men. We see that Nettie's encounter with independent blacks has broadened her idea of opportunity considerably. Even though Celie may not yet realize it, Nettie's descriptions of Harlem empower Celie and they may be a factor in the economic independence Celie achieves later in the novel. The concept of black prosperity and independence is yet another submerged or suppressed narrative that is now emerging into the foreground of Celie's consciousness.

LETTERS 61–69

SUMMARY

*It must have been a pathetic exchange. Our chief
never learned English beyond an occasional odd
phrase he picked up from Joseph, who pronounces
"English" "Yanglush."*   (See QUOTATIONS, p. 47)

Celie's spirits rise now that she knows Nettie is alive. Celie decides
that she will leave Mr. _____ as soon as Nettie returns to Georgia,
and she wonders what her children look like. She continues to read
Nettie's letters in the order in which they were sent.

In her letters, Nettie tells the following story. She, Corrine, Samuel, the children, and their guide, Joseph, travel for four days
through the jungle until they reach an Olinka village, their final des-
tination. The Olinka villagers crowd around them because they are
unaccustomed to the sight of African-American missionaries. One
woman contends that Olivia and Adam must be Nettie's children
and asks if both Nettie and Corrine are wives of Samuel's. Together,
the group is ushered into a hut with no walls, and the Olinka serve
them dinner and palm wine.

Nettie befriends a woman named Catherine, whose daughter
Tashi quickly develops a friendship with Olivia. Corrine, meanwhile, grows increasingly uncomfortable with Nettie's nebulous
role in the family and is frustrated that the natives think Nettie is
Samuel's other wife. Corrine requests that Nettie not allow the children to call her "Mama Nettie." Eventually, Corrine also requests
that Nettie no longer invite Samuel into her hut alone and that she
and Corrine no longer wear each other's clothes.

Because, as girls, Tashi and Olivia are not allowed to enter the
local school, they join Nettie in her private hut to talk, tell stories,
and share secrets. Tashi is the only one of the Olinka villagers who
wants to hear about African-American slavery, and it angers Nettie
that the Africans fail to acknowledge even partial responsibility for
the slave trade. Consequently, Nettie begins to feel that Africans are
just as self-centered as white Americans.

The village soon experiences a turn for the worse when road
builders working for an English rubber company plow through the
middle of the village with orders to shoot anyone who opposes
them. They destroy village homes and crops and force the Olinka to

start paying rent on their own land since the company claims the Olinka no longer own it.

Corrine continues to fear that Nettie is encroaching upon her family and threatening her identity as a wife and mother. Corrine becomes ill with a fever and, wondering if Nettie might really be Olivia and Adam's biological mother, demands that both Nettie and Samuel swear on the Bible that they had never met before Nettie came to their home for help.

Nettie, believing that Olivia and Adam are in fact Celie's children, finally requests in private that Samuel explain how he adopted them. Nettie learns that Celie and Nettie's father had been a farmer who decided to open a dry goods store. The store was very successful and always teeming with customers. Competing white store-owners were furious at Nettie's father for taking all the black business away from them, so they burned his shop and lynched him. At the time, Nettie's mother had already had Celie. Soon after her husband's death, Nettie's mother went into labor and gave birth to Nettie. Though she never fully recovered from the mental anguish of her husband's death, she remarried, to a man named Alphonso, and continued having children until she died.

Alphonso and Samuel know each other from Samuel's wild days, before Samuel became religious. One day, Alphonso showed up at Samuel's door, saying that his wife was too ill to care for their two youngest children. When Alphonso offered the two children to Samuel, Samuel could not refuse because he and Corrine had been unable to have children of their own. Samuel never revealed the identity of the children to Corrine, so when Nettie showed up, both Samuel and Corrine had assumed, from the resemblance, that Olivia and Adam were Nettie's children.

Dazed after learning that Alphonso is not her real father, Celie stops writing to God and begins writing to Nettie instead. Shug decides to move back to Tennessee and asks Celie to move with her. Before they leave, however, Celie wants to go see Alphonso. She and Shug find a new house with a beautifully landscaped yard built on Alphonso's old property. Alphonso has a new wife, Daisy, who is only fifteen years old. Alphonso confirms that Celie's real father was lynched and that he is really only her stepfather. Celie and Shug stop by the local cemetery, but they are unable to locate Celie's mother and father's gravesite because it is unmarked. Comforting Celie, Shug tells her, "Us each other's peoples now," and kisses her.

ANALYSIS

Throughout *The Color Purple,* Walker makes it clear that story-telling and communication are crucial to self-understanding. By this point in the novel, we have seen problems due to failed communication between Celie and Alphonso; between Celie and Mr. _____; among Nettie, Samuel, and Corrine; and between Celie and Nettie. As the novel progresses, some of these ruptures in communication are repaired through narratives of one kind or another. Celie finds Nettie's letters, Samuel tells the story of his children to Nettie, and Celie confirms this story with Alphonso, learning the truth of her own family history. However, aside from communication failures in these specific relationships, Walker highlights many broader, more general communication problems in the world that remain unresolved. She points to failed communication between men and women; between American blacks and American whites, between American blacks and Africans, and between Africans and European imperialists.

Celie's discovery of her true family history brings about a major change in her pattern of communication, as she develops surrogates for God and her parents, in the form of other women. After learning of her tragic background, Celie feels that she has lost some of her faith in God, and closes what she intends to be her final letter to God by chiding, "You must be sleep." Instead, Celie begins to write letters to Nettie. Likewise, though Celie is unable to locate her parents' graves, to which she looks for closure, Shug tells Celie, "Us each others peoples now." These strong, surrogate ties that Celie makes with other women allow her to create a new family in the face of the tragedies she has endured. Celie ceases to wait for the kingdom of heaven and begins to search for peace and happiness in her own life.

Nettie's voice, likewise, has burst forth after being obscured for so long. We see that Nettie has become highly intellectually curious and sophisticated, and is now a missionary, a job that is centered around articulating a narrative. Nettie is very vocal in her attitudes toward the native Africans, especially the self-centeredness she perceives in them, and their clear sexism.

Additionally, by highlighting the self-centeredness Nettie perceives in the Olinka community, as well as its clear subordination of women, Walker complicates her depiction of race and identity. Though the Olinka are oppressed by a colonial force, the rubber company, there is still significant oppression within the Olinka community itself. This internal oppression, coupled with what Walker

portrays as the self-centeredness of the Olinka people and their indifference toward African-American slavery, complicates the seemingly straightforward categories of oppressor and oppressed.

LETTERS 70–82

SUMMARY

Well, us talk and talk about God, but I'm still adrift. Trying to chase that old white man out of my head. I been so busy thinking bout him I never truly notice nothing God make. Not a blade of corn (how it do that?) not the color purple (where it come from?). Not the little wildflowers. Nothing.

(See QUOTATIONS, p. 48)

Nettie confesses to Samuel and Corrine that she is their children's aunt. By this point, Corrine is very ill and has grown bitter and unfeeling toward the children. Still certain the children are Nettie's, Corrine refuses to believe Nettie's story and is stubborn in her belief that Nettie and Samuel are lying to her. Nettie tries to make Corrine recall the time when Celie saw her with her children in the fabric store in Georgia. Corrine fails to remember it until Nettie finds the quilt made from the fabric Corrine bought that day. Corrine finally remembers seeing Celie, but dies of her illness that night. According to Samuel, Corrine forgave Nettie and overcame her fear just before she died.

Celie confesses to both Shug and Nettie that she has stopped writing to God. Shug tries to get Celie to reimagine God, not as the archetypal old bearded white man, but as an "it" who exists in and delights in all creation. In the meantime, after eleven and a half years, the mayor and Miss Millie end Sofia's period of servitude and release her. Though free, Sofia feels lost, as her older children are married and scattered, and her younger ones do not even remember her. Harpo and Squeak now have a daughter of their own, named Suzie Q.

Back at Mr. _____'s house, with all the old crew seated at dinner, Shug announces that she, Celie, and Grady are moving to Memphis. In front of everyone, Celie finally speaks her mind, cursing Mr. _____ and later telling him that everything he touches will crumble until he makes amends for the years of abuse and mistreatment he has brought her. The others are shocked at Celie's defiance. Squeak, perhaps hearing a bit of her own story in Celie's defiance, announces that she will join them and move to Tennessee as well.

Shug's house in Memphis is spacious, luxurious, and beautifully decorated. Celie passes the time designing and sewing individually tailored pants. Shug urges Celie to start her own business, so Celie launches an enterprise called Folkspants, Unlimited. Celie returns to Georgia for Sofia's mother's funeral, and many of her old friends remark on how beautiful she looks. Celie finds that Mr. _____ is a completely transformed man who works hard on his land and cleans his own house. Celie learns that Mr. _____ grew weak and afraid and that Harpo nursed him back to health. Harpo's devotion moved Sofia to return to her marriage with Harpo. Celie also learns that Alphonso has died, which means that her parents' land and home are hers. She moves into her own home.

In the meantime, Nettie and Samuel have married. They have become disillusioned with their missionary quest in Africa and plan to return to America. Before they leave, however, Adam falls in love with Tashi, who has recently undergone the painful rituals of female circumcision and facial scarring, a move to uphold the traditions of her ancestors. In solidarity, Adam undergoes a similar facial scarring procedure.

ANALYSIS

In this section, Walker presents personal religious belief as an important component of a strong sense of self. Celie has always imagined God as a distant figure who likely does not listen to her concerns. She sees God as a white man who behaves like the other men she knows and who does not listen to "poor colored women." This image of God held by Celie—and, ironically, by Nettie, Corrine, and Samuel in their missionary work—is limiting. In thinking of God as an old, bearded white man who does not listen to her, Celie implicitly accepts white and masculine dominance and makes the assumption that her voice can never be heard.

Shug's concept of God, on the other hand, is much more personalized and empowering. Unlike Celie, Shug does not ascribe a race or gender to God. Instead, Shug believes that each individual manifests God in his or her own way. Celie's recognition that she has control over her concept of God and does not have to blindly accept the religious viewpoints that are handed to her is an important step in her quest for autonomy and self-respect.

Celie's assertion of herself comes forcefully in this section. Her defining moment, the speech she gives to Mr. _____, contrasts sharply with her former silence. Celie's assault on Mr. _____ releases years of pent-up emotion and hurt that had been silenced. Mr. _____ tries to counter by stripping Celie of her sense of self, as he has throughout the novel. He tells her that as a poor, black, and ugly woman, she is "nothing at all." But Celie's sense of self is strong enough that she is no longer a helpless object, so she resists Mr. _____'s proclamation, reinterpreting his words in a defiant context: "I'm pore, I'm black, I may be ugly and can't cook. . . . But I'm here." The fact that Celie's speech inspires Mr. _____ to reassess and rebuild his life shows that Celie's attainment of self-respect has truly broken a cycle, not only liberating Celie, but others as well.

An equally important component of Celie's empowerment is her newfound economic independence. Celie's clothing design is a form of creative self-expression, but it is also a form of entrepreneurship and a means to self-sufficiency. Celie has taken sewing, traditionally a domestic chore, and turned it into an instrument of independence. Walker implies that such economic independence is crucial for women to free themselves from oppressive situations. When she inherits her family's old property, Celie completes her independence, becoming a fully autonomous woman, with her own money, business, story, and circle of friends.

LETTERS 83–90

SUMMARY

> *Shug act more manly than most men. . . . Sofia and Shug not like men, he say, but they not like women either.* (See QUOTATIONS, p. 49)

Celie learns that Shug wants the freedom to have a fling with Germaine, a young man who is a third her age. Though Celie is less dependent than she used to be upon Shug, Shug's revelation is painful for Celie nevertheless. Mr. _____ is the only person who understands Celie's pain, as he has also felt the sting of Shug's sometimes short-lived infidelity. Celie realizes that she no longer hates Mr. _____, even after all the wrongs he has committed. Mr. _____ loves Shug, and Shug loved him, so Celie cannot hate him. Celie and Mr. _____ begin to enjoy each other's conversation, talking about old times, their friends and family, and their new discoveries about life.

Nettie writes that her and Samuel's years in Africa have changed their idea of God. They no longer conceptualize God as looking like someone or something. Olivia and Adam have grown independent and outspoken like Africans, and Nettie worries they will get into trouble when they return to America.

The mayor's daughter, Eleanor Jane, brings her baby son to Sofia's house. Eleanor Jane fishes for compliments about her son, trying to get Sofia to say that she loves him. Finally, Sofia tells Eleanor Jane that she feels nothing for the boy, and Eleanor Jane begins to cry. Sofia says that she does feel some kindness for Eleanor Jane because Eleanor Jane had showed her kindness, but otherwise, the pain and racism that Sofia endured prevents Sofia from loving anyone else in the mayor's family. Though Eleanor Jane vows to raise her son right, Sofia tells her that white society will probably make him into a racist nonetheless.

Celie overcomes her heartbreak over Shug, remembering the good times she and Shug had in the past. Celie hires Sofia to work in her clothing store. Eleanor Jane finally learns the full story of why Sofia had come to work for her parents and begins to appreciate Sofia's distance from her. Trying to undo the wrongs of her family history, Eleanor Jane helps to look after Henrietta, Sofia's daughter, and cooks for her. Shug's love affair with Germaine fizzles, and she returns home to Georgia. Shug becomes jealous when she learns about Celie's newly cordial relationship with Mr. _____, but Celie assures Shug that she and Mr. _____ just talk about how much they both love Shug.

Nettie finally returns to America, and she, Samuel, Olivia, Adam, and Tashi arrive unannounced at Celie's house. The homecoming is incredibly emotional for both sisters, who are speechless and weak with amazement. The family gathers on the Fourth of July, and many people remark on Tashi's beauty and how well matched she and Adam are. Though Celie feels old because her children are fully grown, at the same time she thinks, "[T]his the youngest us ever felt."

ANALYSIS

Celie's final letter shows the extent to which her character has developed through the course of the novel. Celie's first letters simply related events without really attempting to understand or interpret them. Gradually, Celie began to make astute observations of others and to articulate and analyze her own feelings. In her final letters, Celie not only analyzes her own feelings, but she has the confidence and insight to articulate the feelings and motives of others. The novel ends with one such articulation, Celie's comment that though her generation is growing older, the family reunion has made them feel younger than ever before. In this way, at the end of the novel, Celie acts as a voice not only for herself, but also for all the characters her age.

By making the act of writing a key element in the process of Celie's redemption, Walker underlines the importance of literacy and makes an implicit reference to African-American slaves, who, forbidden to learn to read or write, were oppressed by being kept illiterate. Celie and Nettie likewise use literacy to combat oppression, maintaining a remarkable commitment to writing over the course of many years because they know their letters are the only link they have to each other. Even though Celie is clearly less intellectual than her sister, she gains just as much, if not more, out of her writing. In this way, Walker asserts that writing is crucial and redeeming for everyone and should not be viewed as a barrier dividing the educated from the uneducated.

Celie's final letter also shows that, like Shug, Celie has formed an interpretation of God that encompasses the entire everyday world. She writes, "Dear God. Dear stars, dear trees, dear sky, dear peoples. Dear Everything. Dear God," revealing that she no longer sees God as a distant figure with which she feels she has little or no connection. Celie's acceptance of Shug's trivial fling with Germaine also emphasizes Celie's growth. Celie still loves Shug deeply, but her confidence in herself is now strong enough to survive a lapse in Shug's attentions. Moreover, Celie no longer sees love as a game of possession and control. Celie loves Shug but does not feel the need to tie her down, as she is confident that Shug will come back as she promised. Moreover, we get the sense that Celie is now strong enough that, even if Shug had not come back, Celie would not be lost.

Though Walker celebrates diversity and difference in the novel, the novel ends with the recognition that not all differences can be overcome. Along with the novel's notable reconciliations, such as the one between Celie and Mr. _____, there are several unresolved differences at the novel's end. Conflicts remain between the Olinka villagers and the whites and between Nettie and the indigenous Africans. Likewise, Sofia holds out little hope that she and Eleanor Jane can ever be truly reconciled. Even Eleanor Jane's eventual understanding of Sofia's resentment is unlikely to change the hard facts of the oppression Sofia has endured.

Walker's implication is that some differences are truly unbridgeable. Her novel shows mutual teaching and transformation as more successful than attempts to appreciate and understand difference. Throughout the novel, reconciliation occurs when characters transform and meld each other into sameness. There are no notable examples of reconciliation that come about due to characters who truly bridge differences with one another. Celie, for instance, reconciles with Mr. _____ not because she grows to understand his different ways, but because her influence transforms Mr. _____ into someone who shares her interests and values. Neither Celie nor Mr. _____ truly bridge any difference, as Mr. _____ has transformed himself so drastically that there is no longer any difference between them left to bridge. Though Walker's view may seem somewhat pessimistic, it is important to remember that, above all, *The Color Purple* is a story of successful transformation. Though some differences and conflicts remain unresolved at the novel's conclusion, we have seen the remarkable transformation of an impoverished, abused woman of color into a successful, propertied entrepreneur who delights in her own sexuality and is enmeshed in a supportive, loving community.

SUMMARY & ANALYSIS

Important Quotations Explained

1. Harpo say, I love you, Squeak. He kneel down and try
   to put his arms round her waist. She stand up. My
   name Mary Agnes, she say.

This passage is from Celie's forty-first letter. Squeak has just returned from an unsuccessful attempt to release Sofia from prison. The prison warden raped Squeak, and she returns home battered and torn. However, Squeak is not defeated, and she makes an important act of resistance when she decides to reject the belittling nickname, Squeak, that Harpo has given her. She insists on being called by her given name, Mary Agnes. By renaming herself, Mary Agnes resists the patriarchal words and symbols that Harpo has imposed upon her. Walker repeatedly stresses the importance of language and storytelling as ways of controlling situations and as the first steps toward liberation. Just as Shug renames Celie a virgin, and just as Celie reverses Mr. _____'s words to say, "I'm pore, I'm black, I may be ugly and can't cook. . . . But I'm here," Mary Agnes renames herself to show her refusal to let the man in her life gain interpretive control over her.

2.   Us sleep like sisters, me and Shug.

In her sixtieth letter, Celie is recovering from the shock of learning Mr. _____ has been hiding Nettie's letters to her. To help Celie overcome her anger, Shug positions herself as a very maternal or sisterly figure who protects and arranges Celie's outside environment and makes sure Celie does not act on her instinct to murder Mr. _____. Nonetheless, though Celie and Shug's relationship becomes more sisterly and familial, the intimate and sexual side does not disappear. In Shug and Celie's relationship, Walker shows sexuality to be a complex phenomenon. Celie and Shug are sexual with one another, but they are simultaneously maternal, sisterly, friendly, and loving.

3.   It must have been a pathetic exchange. Our chief
      never learned English beyond an occasional odd
      phrase he picked up from Joseph, who pronounces
      "English" "Yanglush."

In the sixty-fifth letter, Nettie shares with Celie her sentiments about
the Olinka villagers. After the Olinka have this "pathetic exchange"
with a white man from the English rubber company, the Olinka con-
clude that it is a waste of breath to argue with men who cannot or
will not listen. The cultural barrier between the Olinka and the
English is so vast that both parties readily give up, believing no communication is possible. Samuel later mentions that the only way he
and the other Americans could remain in Africa is to join the *mbeles*,
the natives who have fled deep into the jungle and refuse to work for
the white settlers.

With this discussion of the barrier separating the Olinka from the
English, Walker emphasizes that, though narrative can be a powerful force, some differences cannot be overcome. Cultural complexi-
ties and gulfs of foreignness sometimes render communication
futile. This provides a sobering counterexample to Celie's success at
finding her voice and using it as the key to her discovery of self-
worth. Walker admits that some cultural differences are so great
that there is little hope for communication. Unfortunately, she suggests no solution to this problem.

QUOTATIONS

4. Well, us talk and talk about God, but I'm still adrift. Trying to chase that old white man out of my head. I been so busy thinking bout him I never truly notice nothing God make. Not a blade of corn (how it do that?) not the color purple (where it come from?). . . .

In the seventy-third letter of the novel, Celie recalls for Nettie this conversation with Shug. Celie has told Shug that she has stopped writing to God altogether. In response, Shug tries to help Celie develop a new understanding of God, which involves sidelining Celie's notion of a God who is white and male and with whom she feels she has nothing in common. Shug gently suggests that instead of being mad at God for his injustice, Celie should reimagine God as a figure or entity with which she can more closely connect. Just because Celie's image of an archetypal old, bearded white man will no longer do, Shug argues, Celie does not need to reject God altogether. Shug urges Celie to be creative and to see the presence of God in everything and everyone, as a sort of disembodied "it" with no race or gender. Shug's lesson is part of a greater lesson that argues for reimagining one's oppressors rather than rejecting them. Shug shows Celie that she does not need to reject men altogether. She explains that Celie can have men as friends and that her life does not need to revolve around men exclusively. Instead of dismissing men and God, Shug changes the power dynamic by reimagining them.

5.   Shug act more manly than most men . . . he say. You know Shug will fight, he say. Just like Sofia. She bound to live her life and be herself no matter what.

    Mr. _____ think all this is stuff men do. But Harpo not like this, I tell him. You not like this. What Shug got is womanly it seem like to me. Specially since she and Sofia the ones got it.

Celie recounts this conversation she has with Mr. _____ near the end of the novel, in her eighty-seventh letter. Their words of reconciliation concern the acceptance of differences—in gender roles, talents, and sexual orientation. *The Color Purple* concerns a universe in which traditionally masculine traits such as assertiveness, sexual gratification, and physical strength are present in female as well as male characters. Sofia's assertiveness and strength are virtually unsurpassed by any of the male characters, whereas the nurturing and care that Harpo displays toward Mr. _____ could be considered feminine.

By the end of the novel, a sort of mixing has occurred, as some characters' masculine traits have rubbed off onto more feminine characters, and vice versa. Shug, for instance, learns from and reciprocates Celie's gentleness and care, while Celie picks up some of Shug's sexual assertiveness and follows Shug's suggestion that she become owner of a business, a traditionally male role. Mr. _____ and Harpo, conversely, become somewhat feminized. Mr. _____ learns to sew and to be a good listener, and Harpo cooks, changes his baby's diaper, and kisses his children. By the end of the novel, it is clear that Walker sees fixed gender roles as meaningless and impractical.

QUOTATIONS

KEY FACTS

FULL TITLE
The Color Purple

AUTHOR
Alice Walker

TYPE OF NOVEL
Historical fiction

GENRE
Epistolary novel, confessional novel

LANGUAGE WRITTEN
English

TIME AND PLACE WRITTEN
1982, California

DATE OF PUBLICATION
1982

PUBLISHER
Simon & Schuster Inc.

NARRATOR
Celie (and Nettie at times)

POINT OF VIEW
Celie speaks in the first person through a series of private letters she writes to God and, later, to Nettie. At first, Celie's letters focus only on what she does, hears, sees, and feels. Over time, they grow to include more complex themes and insights. Later in the novel, the narrative shifts back and forth between letters written by Celie and letters written by Nettie. However, the letters from Nettie are still read through Celie's eyes.

TONE
The tone is very confessional and uninhibited, as Celie's letters to God are private, much like journal entries.

TENSE
Present

SETTING (TIME)

1910–1940. Though *The Color Purple* is a historical novel, it never refers to any factual events. There are no dates, little sense of the passage of time, and very few mentions of characters' ages.

SETTING (PLACE)

Rural Georgia

PROTAGONIST

Celie

MAJOR CONFLICT

Celie is verbally, physically, and sexually abused by several different men, leaving her with little sense of self-worth, no narrative voice, and no one to run to.

RISING ACTION

Shug teaches Celie about God, sexuality, and love, and helps Celie locate Nettie's lost letters. These actions enable Celie to find her voice and sense of self.

CLIMAX

Bolstered by the self-confidence she has gained through her relationship with Shug, Celie suddenly lashes back at Mr. _____ in an angry verbal tirade. She then moves to Tennessee with Shug and opens her own clothing store.

FALLING ACTION

Celie returns to Georgia as a successful entrepreneur and finds that Mr. _____ has undergone a personal transformation. After Alphonso's death, she inherits her family's home and welcomes the returning Nettie, Samuel, Olivia, and Adam into the house.

THEMES

The power of narrative and voice; the power of strong female relationships; the cyclical nature of racism and sexism; the disruption of traditional gender roles

MOTIFS

Letters; the rural farm community; colors

SYMBOLS

Sewing and quilts; God

Study Questions &
Essay Topics

Study Questions

1. *How would you describe the relationship between Mr. _____ and his father, and the relationship between Harpo and Mr. _____?*

Both of these father-son relationships conform to traditional notions of patriarchal authority and submission. As the legal owner of the family's property and land, as well as the primary source of income, the father possesses almost total control and authority over the rest of the family. He demands the obedience of his sons and all the women in the household. We see this patriarchal relationship continue in a cyclical nature. Mr. _____'s father forbade his marriage to Shug, and Mr. _____ likewise forbids Harpo to marry Sofia. As the family line continues, the son inherits the father's property and the right to extract the same obedience from his sons.

At the beginning of Harpo's relationship with and marriage to Sofia, Harpo seems almost proud of Sofia's independence and spirit. We get the impression that her fiery personality is what attracted Harpo to Sofia in the first place. However, Mr. _____ threatens Harpo's masculinity by implying that Harpo is not man enough to control his wife. We get the sense that Harpo would probably never have come up with this idea himself if his father had not burdened him with it, a mark of the cyclical nature of patriarchy and male dominance. In suddenly feeling the need to beat Sofia to "make her mind," Harpo succumbs to the pressures and expectations that go hand in hand with traditional notions of masculinity and the role of the husband. However, by asserting their objections and independence, the women in *The Color Purple* break this cycle of patriarchy. Celie's and Sofia's resistance and self-assertion transform Mr. _____ and Harpo, and at the end of the novel, the cycle seems broken. Harpo nurses his father back to health and in turn expresses more kindness than dominance over his own children.

2. *What does the way the community reacts to Shug's illness say about the status of women?*

The women in Celie's church speculate that Shug has a disease contracted through sexual promiscuity. They call it a "woman disease," even though men are equally susceptible to sexually transmitted diseases. The community considers sexual freedom, which represents a goal and prerogative for men, to be a sin for women. Shug's constant challenging of and resistance to this double standard makes her the target of many attacks. Ironically, the same women who berate Shug for her affair with Mr. _____ are the ones who flirt with Mr. _____ shamelessly. Additionally, when Shug later returns to the stage, for her first performance in Harpo's new juke joint, she draws a huge crowd of loving, admiring fans. Showing their fickleness, many of these fans, who were unwilling to take Shug in when she was sick, bend over backward to express concern and proclaim their relief at finding she is still alive.

3.   *Why do the Olinka not identify with Samuel, Corrine,*
     and Nettie on the basis of race?

At the time when Samuel, Corrine, and Nettie arrive in Africa, the
Olinka have not yet personally experienced the hardships and rav-
ages of racism. Unlike American blacks, who saw during the nineteenth century that their race was a stigma to them, the Olinka see
no reason to view their race as such a burden. Therefore, the ideal-
istic preaching of the African-American ministers falls on deaf ears,
and their notions that the native Africans would automatically identify with them on the basis of race prove naïve. Walker's point is
that one's identity is much more complex and wide-reaching than
one's race. Though race may play a part in identity, considerations
of gender, class, culture, and nationality are just as important,
sometimes more so.

Suggested Essay Topics

1. Describe Celie's relationship with Shug. How does it change? What is significant about Shug's last fling, with the young man named Germaine?

2. Consider the seemingly ideal world of family and friends that surrounds Celie at the end of the novel. What are the gender roles in this world like? Do you see any benefits or problems with Walker's vision?

3. What role do you think Sofia plays in the novel? Describe her character and how she contributes to the themes in the book.

4. How are Celie's letters to God similar to the African-American slave narratives collected in the 1930s? How are they different?

5. Why does Sofia tell Miss Millie "Hell no" when she offers Sofia a job as her maid? What is offensive about Miss Millie's behavior prior to Sofia's response?

REVIEW & RESOURCES

QUIZ

1. Alphonso never revealed that Celie and Nettie were not his biological children because:

    A. He did not want to hurt them
    B. He thought he was indeed their father
    C. He wanted their inheritance rights
    D. He promised their mother he would never reveal the truth

2. What drug does Grady enjoy?

    A. Opium
    B. Marijuana
    C. Gasoline
    D. LSD

3. Why is a road being built through the Olinka village?

    A. Because an English rubber plantation is being built
    B. To make it easier for the Olinka villagers to travel to a nearby city
    C. Because new government housing is being built
    D. Because the previous road was washed out in a flood

4. Who tries to convince the warden to release Sophia?

    A. Shug
    B. Grady
    C. Harpo
    D. Squeak

5. Why do Nettie and her family return to the United States?

    A.   They are exiled by the government in Africa

    B.   Nettie has learned about their inheritance

    C.   Nettie and Samuel feel discouraged because they have made little progress in their missionary work

    D.   Adam and Tashi are not permitted to marry in Africa

6. How does Nettie end up at Mr. _____'s house?

    A.   She runs away from Alphonso's house

    B.   Mr. _____ kidnaps her

    C.   Celie convinces her to come

    D.   Nettie gets lost and stumbles upon Celie in her yard

7. Why does Harpo gain weight?

    A.   He develops a sweet tooth and overeats

    B.   His medicine has a side effect of weight gain

    C.   He wants to get bigger so he can beat up Sofia

    D.   He drinks too much at his new club

8. In what context is the color purple mentioned in the novel?

    A.   It is the color of Squeak's stage dress

    B.   Shug tells Celie that the color purple signifies strength and power

    C.   Celie writes that the color purple is one of God's creations and wonders where it comes from

    D.   Celie uses only purple thread in her clothing business

9. What is Celie's daughter's name?

    A.   Tashi

    B.   Olivia

    C.   Sylvia

    D.   Sofia

10. Why did Albert (Mr. _____) never marry Shug?

   A.   His true love was for another woman
   B.   Shug was unable to bear children
   C.   Albert's family thought Shug was trash
   D.   Shug fled town to pursue a singing career

11. Why does Sofia get into trouble with the mayor?

   A.   She pickets outside city hall
   B.   She sasses the mayor's wife
   C.   The mayor mistakes Sofia for a well-known criminal
   D.   She is caught shoplifting food for her family

12. Why does Corrine suspect that Samuel and Nettie once had an affair?

   A.   Corrine and Samuel's adopted children closely resemble Nettie
   B.   Samuel is always happy around Nettie
   C.   Samuel has been secretive ever since Nettie moved in
   D.   Nettie seems inordinately attached to Corrine's children

13. What painful process does Tashi undergo while still in Africa?

   A.   She has a lip plate implanted in her lower lip
   B.   She gets an abdominal tattoo that represents her ancestry
   C.   She undergoes the process of female circumcision
   D.   She and Olivia go through a ceremony to become blood sisters

14. Which of Nettie's travel destinations impresses her because of its high black culture?

   A.   The Olinka village
   B.   Alabama
   C.   Cape Town
   D.   Harlem

15. What is Squeak's real name?

    A.   Eleanor Jane
    B.   Mary Agnes
    C.   Mary Avery
    D.   Squeak

16. What does Celie name her sewing business?

    A.   Folkspants, Unlimited
    B.   The Quilt Hut
    C.   Sewing by Celie
    D.   Tailor-Made

17. How does Shug suggest Celie reimagine God?

    A.   As a white, bearded man
    B.   As a black, bearded man
    C.   As the color purple
    D.   As an "it"

18. Why does Celie move from Tennessee to Georgia at the end of the novel?

    A.   To start her sewing business
    B.   Shug wants her out of the house
    C.   Alphonso dies so she finally inherits her house
    D.   The music is better in Georgia

19. What is Shug's career?

    A.   Seamstress
    B.   Singer
    C.   Prostitute
    D.   Grocery owner

20. When does Shug believe a woman stops being a virgin?

    A.   The first time she has an orgasm
    B.   The first time she menstruates
    C.   The first time she has sex with a man
    D.   The day she turns fourteen

21. What is Miss Millie's daughter's name?

    A. Mary Agnes
    B. Sofia
    C. Eleanor Jane
    D. Harriet

22. How does Celie persuade Shug to stay a little longer at Mr. _____'s house?

    A. She offers to share her bed
    B. She convinces Shug she is not totally cured of her illness
    C. She threatens to rip Shug's dress
    D. She confesses that Mr. _____ beats her

23. Who is Suzie Q?

    A. Harpo and Sofia's daughter
    B. Shug and Grady's daughter
    C. Harpo and Squeak's daughter
    D. Celie and Mr. _____'s daughter

24. Who convinces Mr. _____ that Celie needs new clothes?

    A. His sister, Kate
    B. His son, Harpo
    C. His lover, Shug
    D. His wife, Celie

25. At the end of the novel, Celie decides that although she is older, she feels:

    A. Richer
    B. Happier
    C. Prettier
    D. Younger

REVIEW & RESOURCES

ANSWER KEY:
1: C; 2: B; 3: A; 4: D; 5: C; 6. A; 7. C; 8. C; 9. B; 10. C;
11: B; 12: A; 13: C; 14: D; 15: B; 16: A; 17: D; 18: C; 19: b;
20: A; 21: C; 22: D; 23: C; 24: A; 25: D

SUGGESTIONS FOR FURTHER READING

BLOOM, HAROLD, ed. *Alice Walker.* New York: Chelsea House, 1989.

DIEKE, IKENNA, ed. *Critical Essays on Alice Walker.* Greenwood Press: Westport, Connecticut, 1999.

KAPLAN, CARLA. *The Erotics of Talk: Women's Writing and Feminist Paradigms.* Oxford University Press: Oxford, 1996.

LIGHT, ALISON. "Fear of the Happy Ending: *The Color Purple,* Reading and Racism." In *English and Cultural Studies,* ed. M. Green. London: Chelsea House, 1987.

SMITH, DINITA. "Celie, You a Tree." *Nation,* September 4, 1982.

WALKER, ALICE. *In Search of our Mothers' Gardens: Womanist Prose.* New York: Harvest Books, 1983.

———. *The Same River Twice: Honoring the Difficult.* New York: Washington Square Press, 1997.

A Note on the Type

The typeface used in SparkNotes study guides is Sabon, created by master typographer Jan Tschichold in 1964. Tschichold revolutionized the field of graphic design twice: first with his use of asymmetrical layouts and sanserif type in the 1930s when he was affiliated with the Bauhaus, then by abandoning assymetry and calling for a return to the classic ideals of design. Sabon, his only extant typeface, is emblematic of his latter program: Tschichold's design is a recreation of the types made by Claude Garamond, the great French typographer of the Renaissance, and his contemporary Robert Granjon. Fittingly, it is named for Garamond's apprentice, Jacques Sabon.

SPARKNOTES TEST PREPARATION GUIDES

The SparkNotes team figured it was time to cut standardized tests down to size. We've studied the tests for you, so that SparkNotes test prep guides are:

Smarter:
Packed with critical-thinking skills and test-taking strategies that will improve your score.

Better:
Fully up to date, covering all new features of the tests, with study tips on every type of question.

Faster:
Our books cover exactly what you need to know for the test. No more, no less.

SparkNotes Guide to the SAT & PSAT
SparkNotes Guide to the SAT & PSAT—Deluxe Internet Edition
SparkNotes Guide to the ACT
SparkNotes Guide to the ACT—Deluxe Internet Edition
SparkNotes Guide to the SAT II Writing
SparkNotes Guide to the SAT II U.S. History
SparkNotes Guide to the SAT II Math Ic
SparkNotes Guide to the SAT II Math IIc
SparkNotes Guide to the SAT II Biology
SparkNotes Guide to the SAT II Physics

SparkNotes Study Guides: